About the Author

Ting Ting is an educator and advocate for learning disabilities as she was diagnosed with one at the age of five, and the author of her new book *Leap* taking real events within her life and plotting her story literally in her writing. And whatever unfolds is what life has in store for her; she hopes to share those painful, hurtful, frustrating, hopeful, and joyous moments with her readers to remind people that everyone has moments in their life where they will be at crossroads. That it may feel the world is ending, but humans are strong, and they will survive and push through.

When not writing she enjoys putting herself out there and experiencing the things that life has to offer, from travelling to fifteen countries and counting or sudden lifestyles change like a chance to be a hermit for two weeks.

Leap

TING TING

Leap

Vanguard Press

*Vanguard Press is an imprint of
Pegasus Elliot Mackenzie Publishers Ltd.*
www.pegasuspublishers.com

First published in 2024

**Vanguard Press
Sheraton House Castle Park
Cambridge England**

Printed & Bound in Great Britain

To leap or not to leap?

This book is dedicated to us and to what we were.

Acknowledgements

Acknowledgements go out to all the people in my life that have supported me throughout my journey no matter how crazy the ideas seemed. My mother for trying to keep me alive during my hard times through feeding me food with her gastronomical cooking skills. My father for letting me just be sad for myself and there just watching. My brother and his girlfriend for always being my safe space to talk to. My friends for being my free therapist and allowing me to talk in circles as I wrap my ideas for my novel for months till end.

Contents

Insight

Everyone perceives life differently, from using our five senses to our feelings. As I talked to others about their relationships and life, everyone had a story to tell. Here I am currently writing this book as I reflect on my relationships and experience during my break. I don't know how my story will end, but I hope the lessons that I have learned so far will guide me well. I hope this book will help you learn how to be a better reflector as you consider my questions and speak and listen to your truth.

This book is written in between the second and first person as it is the conversation I had with my inner self. I think one thing about reflecting is talking to that inner-self and asking yourself questions and listening to your answers. Be curious about yourself, research, read, talk to others, and listen to help you find your answers. However, you may never find the right answer you are looking for, and that is okay. Whatever you are searching for, you will be taking a step closer to understanding and finding your answer.

The ideas that I have discovered may not resonate with you, because I am not you. Our personalities, culture, upbringing, and morals are all different, which makes us understand the world around us differently. The experience that I've faced may be the same for many, but our lessons may be different. Some of these lessons and thoughts have already come way before our time. This book is a true story, and I hope to show you how these lessons have influenced my concepts and ideas about life. However, these ideas are always continually evolving as we experience new moments in our life. Place yourself in the story as I have, reflect as if you made the same mistakes as me. Explore the questions I ask and question my ideas to help guide you towards a closer step to your answer. I'll warn you now that you may not get the answer at all.

Know thyself

I was born to two immigrant parents who came to Canada, hoping for a better future. My father was a refugee trying to escape from the Vietnam war. He came travelling across the Pacific Ocean with his eldest brother on a raft. At the age of thirteen, he was alone in a new country, not knowing a word of English. He had to find work, go to school, and sponsor his family of five over to Canada. This is a story of its own, which he loves to tell though, what I always found beautiful was the people he was blessed with in his life that gave him that hope.

My mother was the fifth oldest daughter out of eight kids, and she came to Canada with her family at the age of sixteen. She also needed to adapt to this new world, but at least she was not truly alone.

My parents came from wealthy families back in Asia, but they now had to learn the concept of not being privileged. I couldn't even handle peeing in a hole when I went to China, let alone taking away the privilege of a lifestyle that one only knows. I do not know if I could survive and go through what seems like hell to me, surrounded by poverty where a better future seemed so far away.

Through my parents hardwork and sacrifice they took those little steps towards a better future. I had my own steps to make as my family was not rich, but at least I wasn't as poor as my dad when he came to Canada. My parents offered me what they could at the moment of time and as a child for some reason you can never see the gratitude... I wonder why? Where did my shame come from? Was it because my peers had a better life? They had parents that weren't frugal? Jealousy? Being different? It is strange the transition from when I was in elementary school I was always embarrassed about it, but something happened and in high school I was proud about where I came from. Maybe it was me realizing how exciting this journey was that I was on with my parents. Or maybe it was because my family finally reached middle class? I do not know what triggered it honestly, but I love telling this story about my parents and how I came to be now

My parents were strict with me, but I wouldn't be where I am today without them. Back in the day as a teenager, I had so much anger towards them. That all my friends could go out to parties, and their parents gave them money to hang out. While here, I was questioned whenever I asked to go out. I stopped asking because they got so annoying, the nagging and lecturing about the same thing, about how to be safe, scared that I was hanging out with the opposite sex, and constantly worrying about me. The lack of trust and honesty, though who can trust teenagers? Though maybe because my parents still haven't taught me everything they knew about the world to trust in their own parenting skills? To me, my friends had freedom. Though I also know that most immigrant families pride themselves on education as the exit ticket to poverty and a better life. The belief that only in Canada/America can class mobility be real as education is the great equalizer. Though there are so many others reaching for this dream, my parents knew that I would need to do much more to increase my chance of success. At the age of seven I remember crying my eyes out as my dad took away all my toys, including my stuff animals, because *"It was time for me to focus on my studies."* I remember that day as probably the worst day of my life at seven! They wanted me to be well rounded and talented, not only in school but also in sports, culture, and music. When my parents started to make me work at thirteen, I ended up experiencing adulthood a lot earlier, learning how to save my money, dealing with work situations, and gaining work experiences. My parents aren't perfect, but they tried their best. My childhood and youth kind of sucked at that moment, but for the future it became less limited, so I thank them for that.

A lot of the things that were "mine" during these years were hand-me-downs. If I could describe my look, it was trying to make plain office attire — from my aunties who were all thirty years old — fashionable. At one point it got so bad that when I grew taller than all my aunties I had jeans that would reach my ankle and I would pair them with white sport socks. I tried creating my own style in high school and I got sick of the look and would secretly buy clothing from the mall, but my parents would always get upset at me spending my money on "useless" things. It is probably why I now have an amazing closet filled with some very nice things. Honestly, I think it became an addiction for me to have nice things since I could afford them now that I'm older. To have the latest fashion style, but I also know a part of me has always enjoyed fashion and styling clothing.

Back to the point of this moment of my life, I just felt that every little thing I did was wrong and a disappointment to them. I didn't even do drugs, drink, was always on top of my studies, worked, but just the simplest things were something that got them mad at me. I knew how hard my parents worked and I think a part of me was just trying to be the best for them. I put it on myself to be perfect for them, though I think that got the best of me. A turning point in my life at the age of seventeen was deciding to go very far away to university. I knew what I wanted and needed at that moment. I wanted to go far away to get my freedom from my parents. To go out to parties without question, explore the world without my parents' eyes watching me. To buy the things I wanted without being asked questions. To date without hiding it from the world.

Gosh, that was one of the best decisions I made for myself. I faced all my fear, and I went for it. I went into debt, I had to work harder, struggling was hard alone, but even so I was happy.

My parents are sometimes closed-minded, and sometimes that limits them in seeing interactions more than it may seem. Their experiences have been so harsh and hard, that they only know the world at its worst. I can understand that and the person I am today is also because of them from all the good and bad experiences they gave me. The struggle, the pain, and hardship, but the joy that all of that brought came to make me stronger. As the saying goes, my parents did teach me how to fish rather than just give me a fish to eat. At twenty-four, I have paid off my student loans, made some investments, have a stable job, and no liabilities.

You would think that I would have the feeling of freedom, but I didn't. I was trapped in my unconscious mind by my parents' disapproval, but worse, my own pressure and disappointment in myself because it was more painful. My life has been about how to fish and it gave me amazing qualities from being strong, resilient, independent, but with these qualities comes an image and sometimes it is hard to keep up. And I'm afraid of so many things in the world. We are all told and know that it is okay to be scared, but it is so much harder to accept it and do it! To admit you are afraid and to understand what this concept of accepting is. Fear you could feel it as an emotion, but it is still a thought and idea, it's both abstract and physical. What does "acceptance" feel like? What does it look like to you? Do you need experience to know what acceptance is? Or can you simply question the idea for yourself, and that is enough to know that this is what "acceptance" means to you? Acceptance has always been such a passing thing for me that it is only later that I realized that I have accepted something, that there are no other emotions towards it, I have simply just been okay with something... maybe that is what it is?

I realized that I would not have the freedom I sought from myself because of my own expectations. I was always a go-getter. In high school, I knew that I wanted to go into biomedical science to prepare for medical school. I joined the volleyball and swim team, volunteered in the hospital, became a yearbook executive, worked as a lifeguard, and maintained a 92.5% average. When I went to university, it was the same: joining clubs, volunteering in a research lab, "trying" to keep up my grades (but failing) and prepping for the MCAT. I remember there was a point in my student life, where I had to think about what I wanted to do. Did I want to become a doctor? Why did I want to become a doctor? What did I want from life?

There was this company that came into class once talking about teaching English in different countries. I thought that was very interesting, and it made me wonder more about the future. I imagined myself as a doctor but then realized that I wouldn't be fulfilled by just saving lives. That wasn't a passion, and there's a lot to consider becoming a doctor and sacrifice that was going to be made. My love for a title was not enough for me to willingly sacrifice other things I wanted to experience in life or put on hold. I wanted to travel and see the world, experience cultures, meet new people, try fresh foods, and have a meaningful career. Not saying a doctor is not a meaningful career, but it's how you find meaning in your work beyond just money. How it makes you feel and that rather than getting tired, it uplifts you. I never hated teaching swimming, and maybe it was because of my co-workers. I had some good times with them. Or perhaps because I liked teaching or that I loved swimming? It was a job for my teenage self, but I never really hated it. It was my first time in practicum during teacher college that helped me find that answer. It was the laughter with my students, the being silly with no judgement, the learning and exploring, and the career that allowed me to be human. Though even when I had to change my occupation, I still had high expectations for myself. At what point was I willing to give myself a break? Though it is hard to escape from your expectations that are also unconsciously driven by society too.

The next thing I knew was that life continued to get busier, and adult responsibilities took over, and I forgot personal growth. Then I started to think more in-depth into the future, and it's only through loss that I got a wake-up call.

Lesson one: Understand your past

When I took the time to understand my past relationship with the world around me, it allowed me to understand the behaviour and actions that I have now. There is a correlation between my past and present and my reactions and why I produce them. For me, one of them was being honest with my feelings. Because of my fear of disappointing my parents, the fear of making them worry, I would hide how I felt and the events around me. This became a habit, so as I got into relationships, I struggled to be able, honest, and express my wants and needs as I would have liked. Judgement was also one, but because it was a fear from my parents. That was because they wanted me to hide my learning disability and the shame of being labelled as "stupid or different".

My parents always told me never to tell people that I had a learning disability because of the stigma. In a way, they wanted the world to see me the same as themselves. Maybe they wanted me to see myself as the same as everyone too. My parents were never ashamed of my disability, but worried about the shame that the world would put on me. This shame made me hide behind this mask or title of being perfect. In high school and midway into university I was trying to be perfect.

For myself, my parents and society. Being placed on the honor roll, getting scholarships, being an athlete, being good at art and music, being a part of many clubs, volunteering and preparing for my dreams and future.

The need to be perfect was exhausting. Many people would say you should forget the past and move on, but I feel the past is too important to ignore. That there is so much that you can learn from the past to help understand the present, which will guide you to the future.

Whenever I reflect on my past, I get a new understanding of a new meaning to something. It's like reading a book a second time, and you realize the things that you overlooked before. The key is to not be hard on yourself when you do reflect on the past, don't dwell in it because you didn't know what you know now. Even if you made the same mistake again, it happens because that's life testing us if we have truly learned from our mistakes.

I think learning to understand my past helped me learn to understand others' pasts and build on that empathy. There was once someone who told me their fear about coming out. That even as an adult they still feared expressing their sexuality to people. That we know there will be people who will accept us, but the fear of that possibility of rejection because there will be people who will not. Though I've never experienced being discriminated against based on my sexuality, I can understand the feeling of where that fear comes from because I also understand the fear of rejection because of my disability.

So how do I pass that fear? In some way during our life we get damaged and however we get hurt, it becomes a part of it. We are all learning to heal from our own past, we are all trying to understand ourselves. The expectation is that we are only human. That we try our best, and there will be a high possibility that we will make a mistake.

Years 3 and 4: The Move and Lost

This book started because of loss and so let's begin with my break of a long-distance relationship of four and a half years.

I finally became a teacher and was ready to move to London to close the distance with my boyfriend. You would think that life was following as planned. However, work started to get hard in that I was losing my passion for teaching. The place I was working at restricted me from being the teacher I wanted to be or could be. How could I, as a first-year teacher, suddenly lose passion when I had so much before? My pedagogy and practices of teaching didn't fit the school. It was hard to behave and act in a way that didn't meet my morals around education and who I was. I struggled to be myself in a place as I wanted to explore the concepts of inquiry-based learning. I knew I wouldn't be able to grow here in my professional career.

Honestly, I felt lied to during the interview. I talked a lot about how I created my lessons, but here they were, this school that was knowledge-based learning. Students sat in rows, and during English class, students were asked to read by themselves or read aloud when called upon. To ask questions taken from the book and work on their worksheets. This was a suitable method, but it could not be a method that was used all the time. Even school would be boring and hellish for me. Moreover, the constant observation was overwhelming. In Canada observations were at max twice a year. This school observed everyone three times a week. How could I improve in such a short time? The fact is that I didn't truly feel that their strategy of teaching was for me, however, I had to do so because I needed to have a good observation. This was stressful for me as someone who was putting pressure on herself already.

I have experienced many work environments, even a director's role, you would think I would be ready to handle any job experience. But it was disorienting because culturally it was all different. The British education system was more linear and traditional and the mindset was so different around it that the impact ran deeper than you could imagine. It was hard to figure out how to express my worth and my value, which I never really had to do. The financial pressure was hard too, when you are coming to a country with two thousand pounds, and I needed to build that by myself. My boyfriend worked hard, trying to find a project for his postdoctoral program for the past nine months in Spain. Things were just hard, and I never had to deal with problems at work or financial pressure all at the same time.

All of this was new to me and like my father I was doing it alone in a new country. Even though he was there…ish, he wasn't dealing with the struggle at work or the financial pressure I felt and the disappointment from my own expectations of my economic achievements. I was too prideful to ask my parents for help because I should be this adult that can handle herself and I shouldn't be worrying them.

One of my biggest fears is not having enough to prepare for the worst of situations. The concept of money was drilled into me since my childhood by my parents. My parents lived in poverty and understood its pains; they did not want that for me. In their world money was a priority when hard times came, they experienced how the funds got them out. One never knows when one will lose their job and suddenly need to rely on their savings if they have any. One never knows when anything terrible could happen, but we all know in some form money can get us out. Therefore, money played a huge part in my life because life is unpredictable, but I wanted to be ready for it somehow. To protect myself and the people I cared about if they ever needed anything during hard times.

Came The decision to go back to Canada, to British Columbia, it was easier to walk away than fight for my worth and easier for me financially. I even tried talking to my work to make less observations in order to protect my mental health, but still nothing was done. I knew going back I would have my worth and it could be easily shown. The canadian education system is where I could explore my practices in inquiry-based learning in primary. I wouldn't need to worry about money because I had a lot saved up there too. The pains would go away; however, that meant my relationship would go back a long distance. Another kind of pain would come back, but it never hurt much because I always thought of my boyfriend as home. The feeling of security and safety, even when I was so far away, I could always go back to him. The school would also be willing to pay for all my professional development courses, including my Master's. I knew that my boyfriend's job would always, in some way, have us move around. I could fast track and get a master to help increase employment opportunities as we moved worldwide. I knew that it would be a lot harder for him to find a job then for me. Maybe it would be best if he settled and found a place before me. We didn't talk much about my intentions to be honest, which is where I messed up. However, I did ask him how he would feel if I left. He told me, 'No one would feel happy when the love of their life moves further from them.' He also wrote to me on my birthday card in November when I needed to make my final decision.

Now it is my turn to see my little bird fly away. Nevertheless, like albatross, we shall continue to progress individually working towards that moment every year in which we reunite and manifest our love. Still, it is not the moment to take my guapa off, because today is your birthday and we have many fun moments to live together and keep in our memories for the years to come!

I thought he would be unhappy like me, but we had done it already, and we would be strong enough to push through another few years together. We were strong together, but maybe I gave us too much credit.

For the first few months, it was good. My work was amazing, and I was learning so much and finally getting my passion back. I was also doing professional development programs to get ahead to be able to teach in high school to gain experience and broaden my job selection in the future.

In May, I knew something was wrong. His texting was off; it was boring and emotionless. When I told him that I didn't get into my master's program, he wrote, "That's too bad." Now what kind of partner writes that? He also didn't write or make me my anniversary card, which we did as a ritual for each other. I didn't want to overreact or be mad because I knew he was going through stuff and maybe needed his space. This was something we argued onback then, about giving him space, and so I did what I should have done last time.

One of our weekly Skype dates I was talking about coming to visit in August because the restrictions from COVID might be lifted. This led to him bringing up the idea of breaking up, he couldn't see a clear future because we wouldn't see each other for a year. He started to plan the future for the first time in our four years together. He never liked to prepare because of his experience, which I tried to understand and didn't push him towards. Though as a crazy planner myself, I always felt I needed to plan for us. I never expressed it, but he knew how mad of a planner I was. So, wouldn't he have ever thought or considered that I was always planning something for us? For the first time in our relationship, he was planning, but for a future without me!

He felt that I was the uncertainty in his life and a limitation because I can't speak French. However, did he not once think that he was a limitation in my life, and I accepted that and kept fighting? I believed we would push through.

In a relationship, your partner's limitations are yours, but the success is also yours to share. Even in relationships with my parents and friends, my success is also to share with them because I wouldn't be where I am without them. That along the way, yes, I did a lot of things by myself, but they helped me get there to continue to push in some way or form. I don't know if it was the world's anxiety and being socially isolated from his friends because of COVID. He always liked to hang out with his friends and go clubbing, maybe to distract himself from his problems. I had always told him not to limit himself and apply anywhere, hoping to let him know that I would follow eventually. However, in some way, something made him lose hope. What was it? Maybe he thought I lost faith in him, but I always believed in him. Perhaps it was COVID, society, life, fears. Though deep down, it was simple; he had lost hope in everything.

A week later, I told him that we should take a break and not break up, and work on ourselves and then decide later, to which we agreed.

Lesson One: Selfishness

I admit in this relationship that I was selfish. Though everyone I know gave me an excuse that it was because I was young, and I had to be. That I needed to be selfish because it was essential to find yourself within your career first. However, just because he was older than me doesn't mean he wasn't in the same boat. I now understand the saying, *You need to learn to love yourself first before you can love someone else.* It's allowing yourself to be selfish so you can eventually be selfless. I knew he was allowing me to do that, but I guess I wanted more and thought that he could wait a little longer before I could indeed be selfless. I knew that I would be sacrificing a lot already with the lack of stability and growing up faster, but I haven't done it yet. It just felt like I had already because it has been in my mind for so long.

Lesson Two: Create Dialogue

Even in a long-distance relationship, one would think that our communication would be astonishing, but communication will always be a work in progress. I find with communication one will never truly get it right because our emotions take over. Our fears prevent us from speaking out no matter what, the anger that makes us say things we don't mean, the excitement that makes us ramble on, the sadness that makes us say negative thoughts, and the list goes on. It takes away our ability at times to listen and to understand.

Communication I found is three things: question, listen and understand, which are all very hard things to do. We should have communicated to each other about our fears and our struggles, even if we felt ashamed and embarrassed in ourselves. Though I understand that it's hard to tell people who think you are confident, strong and independent, you are weak, an image to uphold even to yourself.

My boyfriend would believe that I shouldn't decide based on other people's feelings. I never adhered to that idea because I'm too much of a caring person. That I had my shit together (most of the time) and knew my resilience that I would be able to give a part of me to help people I loved. One of my concepts of love is that you need to consider and acknowledge your loved ones and their feelings. It's a sign of respect that you can either ignore your partner's feelings or do something about it as partners. I think this also stems from my family because my dad never listened to my mother's pain and emotions. I didn't want to be like that, so I always felt that I needed to be better. I know myself to be still too young and selfish for me to be empathic now and that it always comes later. Therefore, I always ask people how they feel so I can be empathic now. However, maybe my boyfriend thought that it should be automatically done to be truly selfless, but I don't understand that yet. If he told me directly not to go, I wouldn't have stayed because the relationship would have been enough motivation. One the other hand when I told him this, he felt that it was emotional blackmail, but for me I saw it as the motivation I needed for me to push threw my dreadful work environment. So where is the line to emotional black mail in relationships? Why didn't I think of it as emotional blackmail?

Lesson Three: Push Each Other

I didn't push him enough. I should have called out his actions and behaviours more so that he was aware of it. However, this stems from my childhood and my relationship with my mom. My mom always kept pushing me and telling me things, but it felt like nagging when it became too much. Negative criticism you could say, but the constant criticism made it feel that she wasn't noticing my effort. I didn't want to make him experience that, but I wish I had done it more to keep him in check. Even for myself, I needed just a little more to keep me in check. There needs to be balance, and a line drawn from where it is a discussion to when it becomes nagging.

As I reflect on my move to Prince George, I realize how leaving brought back so much pain for him. I remember asking about his past relationship, and he told me that his ex-girlfriend and him were to move into a place together, but she ditched him. I did move to London and found a job, but I didn't stay long enough. Maybe this could have been why he may not have found a job within those nine months because he may have been afraid himself. I didn't think about this until I empathized later. However, I eventually left him to go to Prince George and probably made him feel abandoned. He never went much in detail in it, maybe from the pain. Though I honestly wish I had asked more and pushed him to share. Where did he go wrong in his relationship? What did he learn? I did tell him about most of my mistakes.

Though I never really asked about it because I thought I was being kind to him from remembering the pain, I was doing a disservice for us. As his partner, I was supposed to push him to express himself more as this was something that he struggled with. Even if it made him feel uncomfortable, I needed to make him feel comfortable about being uncomfortable. He has pushed me to read philosophy to try to understand the word, and he called me out on all my bullshit, but I never did it for him or even questioned his thoughts or ideas on his ideology of love, relationships and life.

I realized that connection is there because of tension and where there lies tension is growth. Therefore, most relationships that are too similar don't last because there is no growth. It's the tension, the emotions, and the discussions, the problems and struggles that allow us to change. To push our understanding around how other people see the world even if it is not close to your own life. I didn't because he was older than me, and I felt he had already experienced these things in life. I needed to have the courage to push him myself and realized that the stuff he may experience with me the second time around could always be a different experience. For example, it is said that you should read *The Little Prince* three times in your life. Once when you are young, the second time in your youth, and your third time as an adult. Each time these experiences may present themselves to you at different stages in life, and your lessons and understanding of things will be completely different.

Lesson Four: Mountains

I started hiking a lot into the rocky mountains in Canada during this time and I noticed that I would think I was at the top, but I was just at a very tall and prominent ridge. There are many ridges and small hills on mountains that confuse you to think you have reached your summit. Your mountain is a lot bigger than you think it is, and those ridges are the goals that you need to reach to get to your summit, but it's essential to rest on those ridges. I eventually climbed to the top of my mountain and realized I liked the climb to the top, but when I came down, it was harder for me. It made me think about the concept and analogy people used for life and mountains. That it takes time and hard work to climb to the top, but it's all worth it. Though, no one talks about coming down the mountain. Why? Is it less boring? Is it easier? For me, this was a realization that even when you go down the mountain, you always need to restrain yourself, so you don't go too fast.

For me, it didn't occur to me. I accomplished my nineteen years old goal, to travel the world and teach abroad. However, that was not my summit, that was only my first ridge. My next ridge was the relationship, and that I was closing the distance and going to start making a life with my boyfriend. Though, I kept thinking of too many other ridges in life that made me roll down too fast to the next climb without having the skills for it. I think a part of me wanted to grow up faster since my boyfriend was older than me to fit the social timeline. I needed to embrace my success and take it in, reflect on the lesson of my achievement and rest on that ridge. All I know is that the taller your mountain is, the more beautiful the summit will be.

Lesson Five: Independent vs Dependent

The break itself made me re-evaluate what my independence means as this was a massive part of my identity. I was independent in my career, which led me to be independent financially, which led to many other forms of freedom. I had my place for rent and provided for my own needs and wants. Though was I independent emotionally? I was able to self-regulate when I started to feel anxious about the complexity of the relationship, life and the future. However, you can only do so much on your own as those feelings can and will reappear. I did talk to people about the situations I was in, and it was helpful to gather my thoughts. Though the one person I wanted to talk to and tell, I couldn't because it wasn't the right time.

It's hard to hold these feelings inside because you aren't releasing those feelings to the person you want. This is true beyond just relationships of a couple, but the relationship with parents, friends, or work. I realized that we are all emotionally dependent. After all, our emotions appear most of the time because they are being acted on either by people or a situation. That we can only work out our emotions with what is being acted on us, thus our emotional well-being is more dependent than it is independent. There are so many forms of independence and dependence that my identity of independence has changed. I am independent where I can care for myself but being independent also means knowing how to be dependent on people. Thus, I needed to continue to work on the willingness to be dependent when I needed to.

The Beginning

There was so much more to our relationship than just the break, and so let me take you on to the journey where it all began

It was the summer before I started my third year of university. There was a ritual I always did with my friend, and that is going to the carnival in Toronto every year to see a psychic. I never really believed in anything they said, but no harm in knowing what will come, right? One psychic said I was going to be a doctor, but nope, I ended up being a teacher.

I remember us walking down the carnival market searching for a psychic at a reasonable price. There sat a tall, mysterious woman with jet black hair, pale skin, dressed in a tight black dress. She didn't seem to be attracting customers, but there was something mysterious about her. Maybe you can say I felt witch vibes from her, and it was only logical to trust that she was good at reading the future.

As she did my reading, she talked about my future career, but then continued to give me a detailed love reading for the first time. I never really looked for love after my dating experience in high school and the first part of my university year. I played around, but nothing special after my first boyfriend. I was always focused on my career because that's all you know when you're in university and getting ready for the big world. Trying to get those internships that are going to make you stand out on your resume as experience. Doing volunteer work in research labs so that you can say you have research lab experience. Love was the last thing on my mind as I also didn't know where I would be going after four years.

She told me I would meet someone and I asked her when and she said soon. She told me that I would find my one when I was twenty-one, and I was nineteen.

Fast forward a few weeks and I am sitting at an introduction table at the lab I was volunteering at. There were six people at the table, and my professor wanted us to introduce each other and our role in the lab. I wasn't paying much attention to everyone's introduction (I know that because one day as we were running, he corrected me on how to say his name... I was saying it wrong for two months!). When it came to his turn to speak, I remember only getting a glimpse of a purple t-shirt and his rugged beard but went back to working on my laptop. As I listened, he said his name with a weird accent and that he worked with frogs at the lab. As I look back, was this fate already setting me up before the fall? I remembered in the spring before the fall my professor asked my friend and I who would like to work with frogs. I rejected it because I felt more motivated to work with fish. Was fate already knowing about our meeting before I even was aware of it?

After the meeting, I left and went to do some chores, and as I was walking down the aisle at Shopper Drug Mart, I remember glancing at a tall, skinny bronzed man for a second. The next thing I knew, this man stopped me to tell me that I had the most captivating eyes and asked me to go for coffee. This was the first time anything like this happened to me in a non-drunk setting. I thought there's a first for everything and accepted his offer and went to Coco 79.

We sat on the patio with the sun reflecting on our faces and the light wind brushing against my hair. We talked about our careers, interests, hopes, dreams and goals, but I still never really felt a connection. These events with a strange man kept happening, from strangers talking to me at bus stops or stopping me on my way to class for three months, until I realized I may have feelings for my boyfriend. Maybe it was the universe testing our relationship already. Or maybe the chance to see my multiple ones in my life?

Lesson Six: Have A Little Faith in the Universe

The saying, *Don't look for it; it will come to you.* I was not looking for love, but I ended up falling in love. I tried so hard not to! I knew he would be leaving in a year and that we would be in a long-distance relationship for a while as I had at least three more years of schooling, and he was also ten years older. We both knew that there was going to be a challenge if we took this relationship on.

Many people stop a relationship because of a long-distance relationship because we all know how much effort and hard work you put into it. Sometimes you do not have the control over things in life, and we need to accept that. However, the conditions that are given by fate are for us to work out. Fate has given us the challenge of the love of a ten-year age gap and long-distance, but fate has also put two people who would also be starting their careers almost simultaneously and maybe their life together?

I believed that there is a balance that destiny and free will have always worked together. Even before the relationship, this idea was powerful for me as I've experienced it myself. Fate gave me the predisposition of having a learning disability (dyslexia as a phonological disorder). I was so behind in school by grade 6 they told my parents that I wouldn't be able to go far in life, but here I am with two university degrees and a stable career. There are things that we can control in life and things that we cannot, and it is with our will to take what we have and make it what we want it to be.

Friends with Benefits

This is where the fun begins. It was in October, and we were doing our regular workout and I remember doing chin-ups and dying while he grabbed my waist to help me. I usually don't like people touching me, but his touch was different because I didn't feel bothered by it.

After we finished our workout, he invited me over for dinner, and we all know the way to a woman's heart is food. After cooking together, we watched a movie and then I went home. This started to become a routine for us, until one day we got a little too touchy. We ended up having a tickling fight over something during the movie, but I remember coming home that day, all happy and elated.

I called my friend at two a.m. and told her all about that day. To analyze these actions and what they meant because I was that girl with her friends who would examine everything! Even a two-sentence text that would be broken down in three hours to only respond with an emoji.

A few days later, after our movie night, I somehow passed out and ended up sleeping over. I remember waking up being held by him in his beautiful warm arms. I still think he attacked me even if he would say otherwise. I remember sleeping right up against the wall and then woken up by a kiss. This was going to be leading to something beyond a make-out session if I didn't stop it. Did I want it to stop? No. Though did I need it to stop? Yes. Thank god for my nerdy ass personality as I told him I had a mid-term and needed "energy" for the next day as I continued to make out with him. He continued to tempt me as he kissed me, whispering how he didn't have an exam, and that made me want him so much more.

As the strong-willed and strong-minded girl I am, I was able to play it off cool and told him, 'Next time,' and turned around to go back to sleep facing the wall.

I woke up the next day, phased by what happened, that was a dream, right? I remember cleaning up after breakfast, and he came to kiss me as I did the dishes. I was shocked because this meant whatever happened wasn't a dream. We walked holding hands to school until we had to go our separate ways and I went to my mid-term so not ready.

A few days later, after my midterm, we hung out again, and as I did promise, I gave him his next time. It felt right with him, the way his hand felt on my body. The way he made me feel safe and loved, even though we weren't lovers. The spark and the pleasure that we gave each other, and our connection was beautiful. I was also seeing other people at this time, but this felt so much different from everyone else. When we started to text each other more often, I soon recognized a smile that would naturally appear on the face from knowing that he texted back. Even to this day after dating, he still gives me butterflies when I receive a text. I think it's knowing that someone you love is thinking about you. I realized I started to care for him as I wanted to talk more to him. He began to mean something in my life. I tried very hard not to get attached because we would go our separate ways next year, but I knew he was special.

Lesson Seven: Good Tension

After that night, we agreed that we were friends with benefits (FWB) and talked about the conditions as essential to be clear, so no one got hurt or thought that it would lead to something. When it comes to friends with benefits, you must be honest. Talk about the "what ifs" and how those conditions are applied. Everyone needs to be on the same page.

For me I could do FWB because I was good at separating my emotion from the physical sensation. I'm also very reasonable to understand the rules and that if your FWB is even sleeping with other people, you cannot be jealous or upset. I always made sure I never went on dates and would be the one to always call for that booty call. If we did hang out it would be with friends, which eventually happened with my boyfriend and I at the moment of time. Or that there was a purpose for our meeting initially which was to work out most of the time.

When you start getting feelings, it is essential not to be ashamed and admit to that person. Holding that it is just going to hurt you in the long run just because you are afraid to be rejected. This is where the FWB obviously ends though because you cannot do it to yourself to hurt them or yourself. It is also fun and exciting to play the chase and pull game when dating. Though never play the chase and pull game when in a FWB situation! This just causes miscommunication because you shouldn't be tugging on heartstrings. That is maybe one of the most important rules to put in place, not playing with someone's feelings. I also felt that it was easier to actually talk about other people that your FWB was seeing as a reminder that it isn't an exclusive relationship, that you aren't "hiding" anything. Plus, playing the game can be exhausting, which is something that you shouldn't be putting in with a FWB. It's essential to make your relationship exciting, but also, at the same time making it honest. That maybe you are responding two hours later shows to him you don't care, but deep down, you are madly in love. No one knows your intentions, but you must express them and find the balance. Finding that balance means you need to work hard on making that person feel loved, so when you do play the game, that person still feels love. Or maybe we should all not play the game, and have drama free and calm relationships… but we probably can't help and play the game?

The Label

It was around November when I started to notice my feelings. Or that what I was feeling wasn't good and I needed to step back. I didn't want to admit my feelings because a huge part of me didn't want this to go into a serious relationship knowing the hard future ahead.

He went for a week to South America for a friend's wedding, and he suddenly messaged me on WhatsApp. We started talking a lot more during the times that we could, which wasn't great for my statistics' grade. My birthday was right around the corner as I was planning with my friends, my twentieth birthday party, for which we needed to stay up for twenty hours. Though they all said they had a mid-term to study for that week, which is common as November was where second midterm exams start.

As the day of my birthday finally came, that night I decided to Skype with my long time high school friend as our ritual was to send each other gifts on our birthday and Christmas and make a card even if we were 13,000 kilometers apart. As we were celebrating I suddenly heard a knock at the door, and when I opened it there, he stood with chocolates from South America in his hand. My friends popped out from the side screaming

'Happy Birthday!' as they jazzed their hands around him to intentionally tell me that he was my gift.

We ended up celebrating till midnight and opened all my birthday presents, played games, ate birthday cake, took photos and talked to get to know each other. Of course I stayed a little bit later as he decided to sleep over at my place. He actually had never been to my place before until now. As I said I had strict rules for myself when it comes to FWB. I later asked my friends; how did they even invite him as they never met him or had his number. They told me because of the screenshots of our messages that I forgot to blur out his number. They decided to add him on WhatsApp and messaged him on there and come up with a plan to celebrate my birthday together.

Soon before I knew it Christmas and New Year came and passed us as we went to celebrate with our family separately. Of course we were texting again until we finally reunited after New Year. (If you think about it, we've been texting for almost 1642.5 days.)

I remember getting picked-up from the train station and asking my parents if I could do summer school. that I wanted to stay in Ottawa to be with him longer. They looked at me like I was stupid because I wouldn't be able to pay for rent with my summer job.

It was a week into coming back from Toronto to Ottawa, and I invited him to chill at my place, and that was when he told me he loved me. It wasn't the best timing as we were also getting physical at that time, but there was a moment of shock and I held back to ignore what I heard. I was still working out if I really just wanted a friendship and if it was possible in the future to be in a long distance relationship with him. I would say I did love him because he was becoming my friend, but was it strong enough, that love, to be something beyond that. I think when it comes to that transition from friendship to romantic partner that there is a lot that love can give you to push towards something. Is it love though that give you some form of hope for some future with that person? Or is it the reasurance that you need to tell yourself to go beyond your own fear?

Oh, love is so complex with its beautiful mystery that we have so much more to understand and even when we understand parts of it there's still so much more to grasp.

To be honest I just didn't want to accept because I was afraid for the future of the relationship as long-distance is hard. In the past, my ex-boyfriend and I did long distance for a few months. It was honestly one of the hardest tasks any couple can go through, fighting for something beautiful.

Reading week came along, and he invited me to go to Montreal with his friends to the Igloo music festival. During that time, his friend was also figuring out her own relationship. As we were raving and dancing our booties off in the cold his friend suddenly started crying. She started talking about the uncertainty of their relationship. The best advice we could give her was to communicate and be honest with her feelings and what she wanted. Even if there was rejection she deserved to give herself that opportunity to move on and find someone who will want her.

I remember as we were walking back to our room and at that moment we both knew we were giving her advice that we needed to follow through. I can remember that moment being very anxious that even the atmosphere around us was heavy. I remember laying side by side with him on the bed looking deep into each other's eyes and we talked about the future, my fear of a long distance relationship and he gave me the courage to take the chance because we were worth it. He was worth it and I was worth it. February 7th became our anniversary, but I think I truly accepted it on January 28th. He told me that he knew he loved me when he didn't want to do reckless things any more, because he didn't want me to worry.

On January 28th, that day I was finishing up my pharmaceutical exam, and I got a text after eating lunch together. I didn't have time to go home and make myself look decent, so there I was eating lunch at my usual spot looking out at the snowy winter. This spot was my study spot for three years on the second floor of MRN (Biomedical Faculty at the University of Ottawa). Now let me just rave about this spot and whoever decides to go to the University of Ottawa can see why this was the best study location. One, it was all glass on one side of the wall where I would be able to see the business of life. Right next to my table was the washroom and let's say they had the banging two-ply toilet paper and it had an open kitchen so I would be able to cook some hot lunches. It was also the spot closest to the lab, where we would always encounter each other every day. As we sat in this spot and I looked up to see his face, I saw it... matching pimples in the same place. Then I knew it was destiny! Okay, jokes aside what I saw in my eyes was the most handsome man in the world and that a perfect day would be sitting and eating with him.

Lesson Eight: Take the risk and be vulnerable

When are we afraid to take a risk, think back and ask ourselves, why? Why are we afraid of the risk, and where did it stem from? Taking a risk in anything is a hard decision as it challenges our fears. The fears that may have kept us safe, mentally, emotional, spiritually and physically sane. The concerns that have kept us feeling comfortable with what we have in life now. Risk is hard because it takes us out of our comfort zone; it makes us experience frustration, sadness, and impatience. However, what comes out of that risk may be the greatest growth that we will have.

My boyfriend always said that I don't take risks. I think he is wrong because he never stopped to think about how I perceived my risk. I think everyone has their own level of risk and that everyone has taken risks. It's just how you have to see it through their eyes. This is how you see yourself, your intentions and what you make of your actions. I didn't want to regret things in my life. I always saw regret in two ways:

One: was doing an act
Two: was not doing an act.

Thus, the risk is, will you regret doing something or will you regret not doing it in the future? The regret of doing something is a lot easier to live with than regret not doing anything, I find. Depending on the context of course, like maybe regret of running over your neighbour's cat, but that's on its own spectrum of crazy. We can do something about our actions, but we can't go back on the things we never did. Living with regret isn't a fear of mine, but I know it will one day happen. I try not to live with regret in my life, and so I am meticulous about every decision I make.

Year 1: The Distance

The first year of the distance, he was in Madrid, and I was still in Ottawa. It was hard not to miss him as everywhere I went was a memory or a moment we had together. The power of associating a place with a person is wonderful and strange. Even when you jog back down memory lane and something or somewhere will remind you of someone because of just a moment. When I looked at those places as I stepped on that same path alone where I once stepped with him made me smile, knowing that we both were worth fighting for. To put ourselves in this situation because we were in love and we wanted to be together and could see a life with each other.

Long-distance has its pros and cons. The lack of physical touch can be hard, but it is the discussion we had to have about how we were going to have sexual chemistry. When I wanted to talk to him and tell him something right away, I knew he wouldn't be able to respond because of the time difference. However, it's the little things that make you feel love. A text message throughout the day shows that we were thinking about each other. Or a gift sent that involved another phone number, to plan a suprise. Taking the time to have online dates on the weekend to just be together.

We learned to be creative and add spontaneous moments in our relationship. We had code words for sexting or making open letters. The time spent together was never taken for granted, but at one point it felt like pressure too. That you are trying to make as many amazing memories in a short while that you try to also avoid the ugly, letting go of things that maybe bothered you in the moment. Though we soon realized that the time we spent together wasn't always going to be great, we would fight. The long-distance became a fantastic motivation to work hard to have a goal of finally being together. He always told me that I was his motivation, which I never understood because I thought you should be your own motivation, but maybe I'm wrong?

I also got to spend time with friends. I got to be myself and not lose myself as I worked on our relationship. Now that I have done it myself I think it saddens me when people end a relationship so quickly without even trying the distance. To give up because it's hard or not do something because it will be hard. I was that person, and I think this experience changed things for me so that I try to do things now even if it will be hard. Yes, a person can know themself, but no one knows anything until they try. A relationship does take two, having the conversation with your partner and coming to a compromise is essential. I don't regret my decision because I have learned so much about myself, my limitations, and how to continue to push myself and go beyond my boundaries. For me I was good at long distance as I had other things I needed to work on and kept myself busy. I loved him and never looked or cared for other men. He was the only person on my mind every day.

Lesson Nine: Be patient

This is something that he taught me, not that I gave him much anyways. He allowed me to study in the school for three years to complete my degree, even if he wanted us to be together. Though he was also finishing up his Ph.D. and we would be looking for jobs roughly at the same time. I got mad at him quickly and frustrated with him during times we were together. I honestly did some crazy shit. I once kicked him out of my apartment for being late for dinner. I had some "hanger" issues, which is still something I am working on. I now rather than getting angry have transitioned to crying and sobbing. Those acts hurt me, too, because I knew I was childish.

It is so hard to make sure your emotions aren't choosing your actions. I apologized for doing those things, but I still acted on it. I definitely was immature in that moment of my life, but I did much less of it as I grew older. I think the patience of watching my growth is something that I appreciate. He was ten years older than me and had gone through life, relationships and heartbreak. As I am young and still making mistakes and learning how to love, he let me make those mistakes. Now it was my turn to give him patience to work on himself. Though as I was learning how to give patience to others, I was also learning to be patient with myself. That you really sometimes need both for it to work. Being patient with others is done through empathy and understanding. I found that pushing myself to change at this moment and reflecting and realizing the mistakes I've made was a lot harder. Was finding patience with myself harder because of my own expectations? I think this is one question I have asked many and everyone seemed to be stumped by it.

Lesson Ten: Pick your Battles

My friends have always asked me, 'How do you handle your long-distance relationship?' I used to tell them to pick your battles. There are moments and things he did that irritated me so much, but I never expressed it accurately. I did pick on some things that were super annoying, but I was afraid if we fought a lot, it would be exhausting. However, I realized that it is not challenging; it is a discussion. It is discussing with your partner and breaking it down.

I took away opportunities for us to grow even more and for us to showcase each other's love. To talk more about our intentions, our feelings and our fears. Stuff that bothers you comes from somewhere, and you need to reflect on where it stems from. For me punctuality was something that did bug me a lot. It's part of my culture and how I have been raised. Being on time showed other people that their time is important to you. My mother has always been a punctual person, even more than me. She would always make sure we left two hours before the party to account for traffic and without fail we were always the first at parties. However, for him, it was the complete opposite, punctuality was of no importance in his culture. We came to a compromise that he could be fifteen to thirty minutes late with notice, and I would be okay with that.

We are teaching our partners, but it is also essential to allow them to be themselves. I wish I allowed him to do more of that as he did with me. When you have a discussion, it will be hard at first to not get offended and not act on emotions, but it is also okay to step away from the conversation when it gets too heated. Use the time to cool down, and as you cool down, you will be able to reflect more on the conversation as you are in a better state for an open mind. However, you must always go back to the discussion later in a better state of openness. Meaning you're open to hear out how you have been hurting the person, flaws and your mistakes that you make just because you are your own human. No one thinks like you, so you can't get upset if people don't think like you. Yes, there are some common morals that we may all share, but the way we think is always the exception.

Year 2: Our First Hurdle

I was in my first year of teacher college, and it was going great until my family issues started to arise. My grandmother, who I hadn't seen for almost ten years, suddenly wanted to meet my family because she was passing away from cancer. I had already made plans to travel to Europe for two months. My parents freaked out because this was the first time I would be traveling for so long and so far; with my grandma's death coming anytime soon, my parents didn't want me to go.

Growing up in a Chinese household, the community played a huge part in one's life. The social norms and standards must be met, and that would be a way for a child to make their parents proud of them. In my case, I would be disrespecting my father for not attending my grandmother's funeral, but I wasn't someone to cancel plans. At one point, my parents were going to kick me out, which was funny because I could financially support myself, so that method didn't work any more, but I was still scared! For me, my grandmother wasn't much in my life. She could have been a stranger. I have also experienced death with two of my best friends a year after another. Death had somehow become something familiar for me.

I learned to miss my friends but not to be sad for too long. To think about them at times, and that is how I show them respect.

There was a lot of weight on me as I knew changing my plans kept bothering the people around me, my parents' approval, and my parents' relationship had become so rocky in the end after constant fighting. I ended up going on my two-month trip and flying back to Toronto for a day at my grandmother's funeral.

When I found out about her death, I cried for my dad. Guapo during that time wasn't as supportive as I wish he could have been, but there was also a family party for his aunt's eightieth birthday. Though he never really hugged me or held me when I was crying. I think he was confused since I told him that she was like a stranger to me. However, I never told him I was sad for my dad. My dad never got to spend as much time as he could with her because of our family conflict. My grandma did regret her decision, but she tried to fix her mistake before she passed away. My dad lost his mother before he even got to make more memories with her. I cried for him because I knew the feeling of death and never being able to make any more memories. Though I wished he held me and didn't leave me alone, maybe he thought that was what I wanted since that was probably how he would have wanted me to handle the situation with him. His views of death were cold, that it is what it is, but maybe that was his idea just to keep him calm?

After that passed within those few months, I found out I was pregnant. I did tell him that I would need to think about the situation and decide to have an abortion or not. He held me in his arms whispering that we could have Athena or Kaiwen another time (names that I would have liked to name our little ones) when I left for the airport. It is funny how people can think it is simply to "have another one". Maybe that was the oxytocin in me that made me more attached then I needed to be, but it was one of the hardest decisions I had to make in my life.

Having gone through this I think my view of abortion or "choice" could not be even more pro-choice. Any woman who is put in this situation is already going through a difficult time, so that to make it even harder for them, to judge them for it, is just cruel. To have a choice is nice, even if it pains you, but you have a choice, it is nice. There are so many conflicting emotions from dreams and realistic ideas. The image of how your child may look and erasing that is painful. Knowing that this child will live a tough life. Did I want to put my child through this? Does my child deserve this? Doesn't my child deserve a chance in life? Many would think the female is only thinking about herself and in all it is not the case. Where my career is leading, my finances and support will all come down to affecting my child. That in all your child's life is dependent on your own life, so in a sense when making the decision the child is one hundred percent being thought about because that was for me.

When I got back home, I had a lot of things to do from handling my new job to planning how to carry out this abortion without my family knowing. I was a twenty-two years old girl, pregnant, hadn't even started my life yet. I had already disappointed my family enough that telling them I got pregnant was not a death wish I was asking for.

During my time this month I was planning stuff out with my new job role as a director at YMCA, and hiding my hormonal issues, trying to make a decision. One night I started bleeding a little out of nowhere. I was freaking out because this wasn't supposed to happen. What was happening to my body? I texted him, but he never responded. The next day was my grandmother's birthday party, which I had to attend. I checked myself, and I was still bleeding, but it was getting heavier and the cramps of pain started. I kept trying to reach him, but he never responded. I had to call my friend who drove me to a hospital after the party and stayed with me as I was going through my miscarrage to make sure everything was fine. I remember just feeling judged by the nurses that I didn't come soon enough. I even saw "it", the size of my fingernail, like a bean.

I found out the next day that he was at a rave getting drunk. I did block his number because at that moment, he lost my trust. He left me to experience a miscarriage by myself. I had my friend, but I needed more than that.

For me, it was like your girlfriend is going through a pregnancy and you just went wild clubbing. At that point I realized I would have wanted the abortion knowing that he was not someone to have kids with. He was just not a partner, who I could have children with. I loved him enough and children wasn't an aspiration of mine to have; I could be with him without a child. That we could be together even without the typical family life. He left me alone knowing that I couldn't rely on my mother at the time. He lost my trust with my body, health, and heart. I never knew he could hurt me this much. With my emotional pain, realizing that my body can fail me at any time. Finding out that my body may fail me as a woman and accepting that it may be difficult for me to bear children in the future if that was something I wanted.

This is something that I needed to also work on by myself to regain my dignity as a woman and re-define what a woman meant for me. He wasn't helping as he couldn't accept his responsibility and acknowledge that he hurt me; he kept making excuses for himself. He blamed me for "purposely" getting pregnant. He thought I even lied about my miscarriage, that I would hide a child from him and have it on my own. I was so shocked and hurt by the thought that he even thought I was that type of person. We fought a lot after this, and I said some very hateful things. I wanted him to feel the anger, sadness, frustration and hurt as I did. I learned later that it isn't the best way to handle hard issues like this.

We learned what love meant to us, that for me, passion meant not hate, but indifference. We had this huge problem that happened, and we needed to talk it out for a few months, learn to understand each other, talk about our lessons, and learned to love each other again. I saw him grow in this relationship since he kept fighting with me even through all this pain, we stood side by side together.

Lesson Eleven: Acknowledge your mistakes
(We fuck up all the time)

Acknowledging how we have hurt each other in our relationship is essential. He hurt me and I hurt him. Recognizing that we did something wrong because that showed that we were able to understand each other. It also shows our willingness to work on the relationship. The relationship is all about growth and tackling problems. All humans make mistakes, but we can also learn from them and fix them. When we learn from our mistakes, it will be easier to learn how to solve the next problem. It's important, though, that we remember our mistakes. I don't mean to dwell and hate ourselves for our actions, but to move forward with them. We need to remember what we did because it could happen again.

Similar events happen, and it is a test to see if we have fixed them. Remind ourselves of our lessons, and our partners need to check-in and reflect on past mistakes together. Know that acknowledging your mistakes may take a while but work patiently together by asking each other questions about the situation, explaining your honest feelings, and being curious and listening without judgement. Rather than making excuses for yourself, just come out and say how you fucked up. That day for us was June 8th.

Lesson Twelve: In any relationship you will hurt each other

In a relationship with a mother, father, friend or partner it is only natural that we will hurt people that we are in a relationship with as much as they will hurt us Everyone must acknowledge that, but also take the initiative to do something about it. If individuals keep getting hurt repeatedly by the same thing then that's not taking accountability for it. This is my other concept of love: we go into a relationship knowing that the person will hurt us, but it is having that trust and respect that they will catch us. For me, I never thought he would hurt me like he did. That it almost felt like a betrayal with our trust and the respect crumbling to the ground. We needed to patch up the foundation and re-evaluate our weak foundations. What did he need for me to trust him again? What did I need to do for him to feel respected again?

Lesson Thirteen: Forgiveness

This was one of the hardest things for me to do and learn. I never needed to forgive someone in my life as I never experienced such pain from anyone before. In twenty-two years of my life, I never really fought with any of my friends. Whenever my friend hurt me, it was something I always tried to understand. I never needed to forgive my parents because I realized whatever they did was for my benefit. Yes, they could have had a better parenting style and approach, but my parents had their cultural understanding of parenting. They only knew the strict Asian style of parenting of tough love. My dad practically became an adult at thirteen, so what did he know about what it meant to be a child?

Why was it so hard to forgive him? Was it because I couldn't understand him? Did understanding someone give that person the key to forgiveness? Is this any different from the fact that even though I could understand someone it didn't mean I can agree with them? I couldn't come to understand his actions with the situation of my miscarriage. Even when you think about those whose loved ones fall victim to crime and injustice. I wonder how some people can find some form of understanding of the situation to forgive. What

I do know is that when you don't forgive you are holding in a lot of emotions still. You are holding on to something still, the feelings of maybe anger, sadness, revenge, frustration and that was me. All I knew was that I was hurt. I tried to Google the answer, "How do you forgive when you can't understand?" but there was no real clear answer which made me feel that I must let go of the pain.

I asked myself, is it something that needs to be earned? Is it something I do for myself to be free? Is it something I do because of unconditional love? Is every situation going to be a different reason for forgiveness? Forgiveness for me was given by learning lesson ten, that I will need to forgive him in my relationship constantly from making new mistakes. That I am allowing him to hurt me, and that is also on me. That he will hurt me not intentionally, but because he will make mistakes and fail, that will hurt me indirectly as he grows to his best self. This would also apply to me, but the key is accountability. That I'm only allowing him to hurt me if he is accountable. Another concept of love I learned is being patient with the people we love and helping them become their best selves even if those mistakes hurt us. It is selfless in this sense that you allow people to hurt you so they will learn something in life to leap forward and be their best selves. It was easier for me to forgive when I thought this way because I knew what was coming.

The Purpose

We all know that quote, *Everything has a purpose in life*. Yeah, that's true. I found myself recognizing that in Prince George, I had two purposes. One was for my career, and two fast-tracking my life for him. I knew our lives in the future would be him travelling because he was a researcher, so I thought that I needed to get ahead in my education so it would be easier for me to find a job. I did not want to be an economic burden.

In London, I also had two purposes. One was starting my career, and two was to begin to build a future with him.

In Prince George, I lost my purpose, him. In London, I lost my purpose in my vocation. Mentally, emotionally and spiritually, I was in pain, which in turn affected me physically. Now, which one was the hardest to lose? Him. My purpose was stripped away from me, I honestly felt lost. I never lost purpose before and it honestly sucked balls and I can relate to the people who start to lose their purpose for whatever reason. Just lost because you're stumped and just trying to find something that makes you just feel something new.

I learned that we focus so hard on finding a balance, but life does not let you do that ever. We need to learn to work with the unbalanced nature of life. I was trying to realign my purpose and compare it to important purposes in my life and found that it was like a spectrum. That your purpose is supposed to make you feel constant emotions, but no matter what there is passion that keeps on pushing you because there is no end (well that is what we hope for).

Your purposes in life will always go up and down. Not all your purposes are going to be met or achieved at once and it's really deciding on a priority, which also changes. Sometimes you can have your priority on work because your relationship is doing well and then that switches and you gotta keep on changing. There is always one that is going to be greater of a loss.

I realized that my purpose was happiness and it never wavered much in my life. I lived in a bubble where I had plans that always worked out, and I didn't need to worry about uncertainty. It made me wonder if my purpose has to be finding happiness. Why are we always striving for happiness? Can we truly achieve happiness? Everyone strives for happiness, to live and do the things they love. Though that would eventually become mundane, don't you think? As life changes, you change and eventually, what was once happiness will become routine.

When I look at my parents and how they started with nothing and ended up with so much. They worked hard for that, but now that they are older, they are still doing that. At first, I never understood why my parents still save like they were poor when we weren't any more? It's a habit; it's what they've only known in their life, and that is something that I couldn't allow myself to be. That they achieved so much for themselves; they are the picture of the American dream. The things they did to reach happiness have now become routine, and happiness just passed them. Happiness is a moment in time, so we will never achieve it because we constantly need to search for that moment. As they say with pain or anger don't hold on to it, I found that it's the same with happiness don't hold on to it... because it is no longer happiness.

Lesson Fourteen: Finding your purpose

Where do I go now? What is my new purpose? What is important in my life? These are important questions that I needed to ask myself to find my purpose again.

In London I was miserable in the sense that I hated my job and that my person didn't move to make it feel like we were starting a life together or what it would look like.

In Prince George I was fine. I liked my job, but it was hard to not miss my partner. I wasn't happy, I wasn't sad, I just felt content and I liked that feeling.

That this is how I wanted to just live for now, with contentment. What did I need to feel content? I must experience everything in life by embracing the pain, the sadness, the anger, the laughter, the happiness, and the will to keep on fighting because that is living. I needed to face the uncertainty knowing that I would be able to face it head on.

When I talked to the older people in my life they shared many stories, but in some way they all started with hardship, which led to some form of contentment for them. Even if it wasn't the ending they were hoping for, their emotions of those events were still there, but at the same time they were content with the result knowing they did their best. For me that showed me they have lived well.

What was important in my life? I realized that my feeling of home was a huge important aspect of my life. I didn't have that any more as I made him feel at home. What's the point of preparing for uncertainty and disaster when you have no home to begin with? This concept of home had a huge impact on one of my fears. Knowing that I needed to find this feeling of home meant I needed to search, but where? I always struggled with home. I moved around so much and with technology it helps with still staying connected with people in my life. I always wanted to explore and travel at a young age and I think maybe it was because I was searching for home? I liked Canada. It was amazing, beautiful nature, had cities, good food, my family and friends, but a part of me felt I didn't belong. That I wanted to experience more things beyond forest and lakes and tall skyscrapers, at one point it all got boring for me.

When I analyzed my feeling of home I had only one thing for certain, which was my garage. My garage was my family in Canada where I store all my shit. I love my family, but at the same time I wanted the life of independence. To go explore the world without asking. To just do my own thing and have my own life separate from my family. So staying and living with my parents was not an option whereas for others it's the best feeling to be with family. Though for me it wasn't just that, probably because of how I saw things. I wanted things to be a certain way for me. Have my own habits in my house, my own self-expression in my decore or furniture to and be truly myself.

My current abstract house in mind was broken and all I had was my garage, which we all know is something you can't live in forever. He was my home. I made him it, because it was like that in some sense, but to be honest it was a beautiful ass mansion. It was now more like a hacked down farmhouse, but I was content with it. So what if I never met him, what would home be like? Well people would say it's the people in your life that make home. Well my friends were all over the world, so they didn't make it home. I knew home with my family would drive me completely insane as we love each other, but we worked better apart. So, what was my home if it wasn't him, my friends or my family. What did home mean to me? What are things that encompass a home? What questions did I need to ask to find my answer to home? Is it where home is? Is it what home is? Is it who is home?

Support

The people around you can help you feel less lonely. Even if they weren't my best friends, parents, or acquaintances. Opening up and talking about my feelings helped me collect my thoughts and ideas to express myself. It was a way for me to admit my feelings and acknowledge out loud how I felt. I had so many people from all over the world supporting me everyday. Phone calls sometimes just on the other side were enough for me not to feel lonely. I was very much an ambivert. I was always good with staying at home and reading a good book all day, but also was sometimes down for a good party with friends. I think what is nice about having a partner is that it is someone you always have in your life that plays a much greater part of it than just your friends and family. Your friends and family as you grow older will start to have their own life, but this partner in your life is someone who you share your life with.

This makes you feel significant. The willingness to do things with you, as you do for them. So for me when that was taken away from me I admit I felt lonely. Not alone, I have been alone within my relationship many times just because of the distance, so why here I was alone again, yet why did I feel lonely. I think it was because I knew I had my person, but I didn't any more. I wonder for those who end up not having a partner what is their key to avoiding loneliness? I think many think that being alone leads to loneliness, but I don't think that is the case. I've also experienced being in a relationship and still felt lonely during my miscarrige.

So what causes this loneliness? Reminding myself about the relationship and the significance I did play in the life of people did make it easier. I knew I wasn't a huge part of it, but I was in the thoughts of my friends and family. They really pushed me so much during my hard time that I wouldn't have been able to handle the busy life schedule for those two months without them. I was working a full time job, doing course work online, and handling my crazy emotions. Appreciate the connections that you have made with all the people in your life. Even though I was in pain, the connection that I kept on growing with the people in my life made it less painful. I knew two things at this point: One, I wasn't afraid of being alone because you are actually never truly alone, but what I am afraid of is loneliness. Two, I knew I needed to fix the connection and relationship I had with my family.

Family: This was my first real long term relationship, of course my family met him. Obviously in a long distance relationship he did not bond as much with my family. Though then again he could have tried and put effort himself and taken initiative like I have. Maybe this is where my empathy and understanding comes in too much?

With my family I was never truly open about my feelings because I didn't want to deal with how they would react to things. I also didn't want to worry them or make them feel disappointed. I think that is one of my reasons why I don't open up about my feelings easily or hard to express myself fully. My parents were different in morals and thinking just because of their own experience. When my father went back home to Vietnam and China, I asked him did it feel like home? He told me China felt close to home, but not really.

Culturally my father has the ideas and values brought up at the time of the Vietnam society during war times and when he came to Canada he had to learn to trust and understand how to integrate into his new home. So when it came to bringing me up I felt also completely lost. I struggled with my own identity as I was not really fully Chinese, didn't even speak a word of Vietnamese, but was also extremely western. One thing I thought was overwhelming was the eastern community mindset and I thought that brought on so many social standards and so much pressure.

My parents were still very much like this, especially my mother. I was afraid to disappoint or worry them because I don't fit into the social standards that they have. I told them I didn't care, but I wasn't honest with myself because I did care. I think expressing it now makes it easier for maybe other to understand me more. Allowing myself to understand my own actions and reactions to things. This is something that I will need to take time to change, but I think the first step is to be honest with my family.

I knew in July I would need to talk to them about the truth of my intentions of going back to London even if I would hurt them. Having my family help me was needed. My mom would call me every day and check in. Knowing that I had my roots made me feel like I still belonged to something and I wasn't lonely.

My parents actually understood me when I told them I didn't want to work in Prince George any more. My parents supported me even if they didn't agree, they just wanted me to be happy. I think my parents have always worried about my mental health since university when I had my first mental breakdown because I was failing calculus. I think they realized the pressure I put on myself, maybe they felt guilty about that.

I always had moments when my parents would annoy me and nag, which irritated me so much, but as I grew older I realized it is coming from a good place. It's having the conversation with my parents, telling them to stop, because it's frustrating at the moment. It's letting people know about how you are feeling in the moment and how their actions may irritate you. Don't let your frustration get the best out of you, take a breath and express your struggles. Don't be afraid to say you can't have this conversation at the moment because your mind isn't in the right place. Though also remind people you aren't running away from the problem, but you want to make sure you are in a good place to have a proper conversation.

I practiced this with my mom on the phone when we talked when I was telling her a little bit of my decision about London. We didn't yell and we just listened. We reminded each other and told each other at that moment how we felt so we were aware about what was happening in the current situation.

I realized that I had amazing parents and I never gave them the opportunity to be there for me. I think I never let them because I still resented them still for their parenting style in my childhood and youthful years. My lack of trust in them because they never showed me that I was good enough in my own eyes. That my parents have changed for awhile, but I never saw past my anger, they are different from when I was a child.

I know that this may not be the same for everyone and their parents, everyone's relationship, even your own siblings', will be different with your parents. This is the first relationship you ever build in your life that starts with love. Even if it may be broken for whatever reason it does not mean you aren't capable of love, but it's working within other relationships you form to gain the skills that you would have developed within that first relationship. I think no parent and child relationship is perfect because you can't teach everything about love within that relationship.

My parents only had their own understanding of love from their own experiences, which they passed and showed to me. When I think about it my Father never had a father to show love or a mother who abandonned him. For my father, being there and providing for me was love to him. My mother had strict parents herself and accepted that as love and showed that to me. But I'm not my parents and for me their acts of love wasn't love to me and how would I have known that as a child. It's only now as an adult I'm able to accept and understand their love.

I'm definitely still learning about love within my own relationship with my parents . That my parents themselves are reconginzing that their way of love isn't the way I understand love and are learning how to love. It's asking yourself, what did I learn from my parents? What do you like and don't like? What you can understand from their behaviours, and what are you missing within that relationship? I think even with all these questions we never stop learning how to love.

Lesson Fifteen: Stop Assuming

What I have realized not only with the relationship with him, but my family is that when you assume you strip away opportunity for people to learn. Thus, assuming stops growth within a relationship. It's hard not to assume, but instead I needed to tell myself "let's give them a chance". Even if my assumptions were correct it's having a conversation with that person that will lead to growth. That is also a part of love, giving chances, because working on yourself and growing is progress, it takes time and it is hard.

Friends: I always knew my friends were powerful, wonderful, and amazing. That I always had a fantastic and supportive group of friends that inspired each other with our beautiful minds. It's because when I was younger I never tried or thought I could have that concept of free judgement and understanding from my parents so I obtained it from my friends. They always brought the joy and the humor in life again. Though as most of my friends were far away I had to get my physical support from my roommates. Two guys who loved the trees, the outdoors, and beer. Though it was a short time we spent together we did many things, experienced new things together, laughed at each other and listened to each other.

We made a connection and this simple connection made me think about the saying "people come and go in our lives". People do come into our lives, but I don't think they simply go. It is putting in effort and working hard that makes someone stay. When that is gone then people leave to find other people that will continue to build a connection. I think one of the most beautiful things in life is the connections that we build and keep.

There's this hilarious moment I remember with my roommates that made me really laugh for the first time. I remember telling one of my roommates how I hadn't eaten for three weeks and that I'd been losing muscle mass. Then my other roommate stopped the conversation, telling us that it had only been a week and a half. It was like a scene from *New Girls* or something, with my stupidity. We looked at the calendar to see if he was correct and he was. That made me laugh so hard because I knew I was letting the pain get to me.

My roommates made me laugh almost every day, even when he asked for a break up. Initially I came out of my room crying. I thought eating would make me feel a little better, but it didn't. My roommate watched me ugly sob and eat ribs for at least an hour, which then he asked me if he could go. In that moment I realized I wasn't alone, while my friends sat silently and listened to me cry for weeks. They listened to me talk about the same things for months on end and they never left and they never told me to stop. My friends who I called every day to talk about my book, the letters I wanted to write to him, and always listening with care. The best thing about my friends is they always question everything with no judgement to help me think about other things and see different perspectives, but at the same time I need to also be true to my story.

Lesson Sixteen: Only you know the truth

It is our perspective and our feelings. They can sometimes be incomplete or wrong, however, our friends and family don't know that. They feel the need to understand us and be on our side (most of the time). Even if you don't know the other person and what their side of the story is and how it felt for them. We need to be truthful to our story and what is missing in the story. What is the point of view that you are not willing to see in your own story?

For our story I knew the pain that I caused him. I knew I wanted to keep on fighting, but my friend worried that he didn't. However, a part of me felt that he also had a little more fight in him. The fact that we still texted each other, he Skyped with me, that he wrote me good morning and good night sometimes (we used to do this every day), that he still used our pet names, that maybe he also had still had hopes like me.

My friends and family cared for me and worried for me and understood that. There were many people in my life that thought this was a stupid idea and that he wasn't worth it. Who knows, maybe even you guys are thinking the same thing. Though all I knew was that I wanted to try and that I knew the possibility was already fifty percent. Okay, maybe even twenty percent, I did fuck up pretty hard, but I was prepared for both possibilities and would be fine with both outcomes; both paths would help me grow into something better.

I've always been a silent lover in all my relationships because of knowing this one thing. People can get into your head even if their words are coming from a good place. Those worries are their fears for you, thus, those fears will be projected onto you and your decisions. Questioned more rather than giving an answer or stating my own opinion, unless they asked me or I honestly stated it. At the end of the day you need to make the decision on your own, not because of anyone else's fears, but your own insecurities.

The Decision

There is so much more background information about our relationship which I haven't discussed. Such as the crazy things I did to him and arguments that we got into during our four years, which led to many essay papers. Relationships are hard even if you are with a new partner or a current one. In each relationship you get in you will have different or similar challenges and experiences, but at different times. The question to ask each other is do you want to continue these challenges that will appear in your relationship with each other? Our relationship's current challenges are the distance and finding ourselves in our career. We talked at the end of May and broke down the problem in the relationship. I decided to move back to London to try to fix problem one, as that was something that I could currently fix, but problem two was him. We decided to try that, but still we were on break until September to talk about problem two.

Lesson Seventeen: Remember your Lessons

I needed to make time to remind myself of my life lessons. Every day we are living and living in a moment and each of those moments we feel and experience give us a life lesson. To recognize in that moment my feelings and ask, "Why do I feel this way? What does it mean? What does it relate to?" Whenever I got nervous or anxious about the future of the relationship, I would work on this book and it made me be present in the moment. Those moments when he read my messages, but didn't respond, which led me to create that thought that maybe we were going to lose our connection by September. Those moments were for me to practice my lessons and growth. This book gave me time for myself to grow to have patience in myself, to have faith that everything will work out, and to slow down.

- Selfishness: It's my turn to do something selfless for him in the relationship. Society places this concept of marriage and that one should only do these selfless things for someone if they are married. This is something my mother would tell me. This was my mother's fear for me, that I wasn't going to be protected by the law or held to some signed contract. Her fear transitioned onto me a little as I grew older. I wasn't truly selfless in the relationship as much as I could be. I remember always believing that marriage is the same as any relationship. The reason you are in a relationship is that you want that person to be your lifetime partner. Does marriage need to represent that you are life partners? Or is it just trust that this person will never leave you?

- Faith: With all that was happening I knew faith would be playing a part in this relationship. Was faith going to break us apart or was faith trying to make us stronger? First, this break happened during May when schools in London were hiring as it was the date for teachers to give schools their termination letter. Secondly, because of COVID, it would be difficult for us to meet other people. Thirdly, I had one more year to use my visa in London before I needed sponsorship. Faith gave me new conditions in our relationship in which I had to now decide what I would make out of it. We took that chance in the beginning together to a long-distance relationship. We both worked extremely hard for our relationship. He gave me the courage to take that leap in the first place. Now it was my turn to take the leap of faith myself and give him the courage to continue.

- Risk: This break was my first-time question. Is this regret that I feel? Did I regret the decision of Prince George? For my career, it was a great decision, but for my relationship it wasn't. In the first few weeks it felt like regret, that I could lose an amazing person and a great relationship because of my choices due to greed and my fears taking over. Though as I further reflected and started to think about the outcome slowly regret faded. I met a lifelong mentor, made new friends, learned more about what it meant to be a teacher, explored my pedagogy, that feeling of good pressure at work. The break in my relationship was to help me grow to become a better person for myself. That this break if we did get back together would make our relationship even stronger and more meaningful as I learned to come to appreciate more of the relationships I built. I learnt more about life and reminded myself of things I already knew. Though I do regret the pain that I caused him. That time I was the one who hurt him. I need to take accountability for it. I needed to make this right for him. I need to show him I love him. I would need to take the risk to go back to London to shorten the distance, without even knowing if we would get back together. This was honestly the only way for us to continue the relationship as this was the first problem of the relationship. This would also be the regret of maybe missing out on "the one". I always believed that as long as I knew I put all of myself into something and tried my best, then I would have no regrets. I tried my best in London so I moved, now I need to try my best in the relationship. The move to London for me was simply a new chance on a second chance. Though I needed to prepare also if he didn't want to take me back so I needed to tell myself this was also a second chance for our relationship or a second chance for me to fall in love with London.

- Slowing down: I knew that I could kinda solve problem one by moving back to London to have a shorter distance. However, the future had changed. He wanted to go and work in France. However, that future could be short depending on how long his contract at work would be. I think he was thinking too far in the future now too, the same as me before. I realized that the future is never fixed, it can change in an instant. My future so far has been quite constant for me. I never had fluidity in my future until now. For the past six years of my young adult life (seventeen to twenty-three) I knew that I would study, work in the summer, and travel in May to June. I think in a relationship you should plan for the future, but don't look at things as end goals because it's an adventure. It takes away the fun in the relationship. In relationships, think about the factors that are uncontrollable and find solutions around that and work around a short time frame. Constantly ask each other: What has changed? What has been accomplished? Can we move forward now? What are some new solutions? I had hope because I wasn't planning for far ahead in my relationship any more.

- Speak your truth : I knew I still loved him. I still felt that we had such a bright future together, that we could make this work. This time knowing our mistakes and working on them together is what I loved about the relationship. Our relationship was what love was. It was great at times, but also really hard at times, this is what true love is. This was real love.

- Purpose: My purpose is to find my feeling of home. I need to see if he was my home or was an attachment. If the feeling of home isn't actually the people in your life, but something much more abstract. I needed to find my answer to my feeling of home. I needed to know if he was home.

Words that were Never Sent

These letters and text messages are actually the early forms of my reflection and how it led me to start writing this book. Though I don't know which is more sadder not sending it because my fears have taken over or sending it and having my letters be misread. These were also letters from my emotions. Writing these letters helped me to figure out my own thoughts and ideas. What was I feeling? Why am I feeling this way? How was I experiencing life at that moment? What question did I need answers to? It allowed me to act on my emotions, but this act would never hurt anyone or lead to further misunderstanding, because it was only the act of writing. It also allowed me to be patient with myself, deciding to send something or not, because either way I was swinging like a pendulum moving back and forth from fear and hope.

Letters Never Sent

Dear Guapo,

It's already been a month. It's been hard for me on some days and manageable on other days. You are my first real long term relationship in which I wanted to marry you and you knew that. We almost brought a life on Earth together and I talked to you about my proposals. This space has opened a future where I may not be with you and that is something that it is hard for me to cope with. It has opened my eyes into realizing how important you are. The potential for not being in each other's lives is hard for me to envision. When I try to talk to other people I miss you and only think about you. Even after four years, when you first WhatsApp messaged me all the way from South America, those butterflies still are there when I get a text from you today. I actually started writing a book and reflecting about each year so far. I'm in the first year and that happiness we had for three hundred and sixty-five days.

- Have you ever taken a break with your other partners?
- Why are you willing to do this with me?
- Do you feel this way too about the potential of not having me in your life?

Lessons I learned so far…

1) I found myself recognizing that in Prince George I had two purposes. One was fast-tracking my life for you. I knew your job would involve us moving around the world and I did not want to be an economical burden; I wanted to be able to also support myself. Thus, I need a higher education and second to work on my career. London also had two purposes. One was to start

to build a future with you, two was my career. In Prince George, I lost my purpose for you. In London, I lost my purpose in my vocation. I am young and stupid I don't have the experience to realize this until I make the mistake. I know which one was the hardest to lose and that was you. My other fears and worries mean nothing more than the bigger picture. I am young and stupid, but I think one of the things I do know is how to reconginze my mistakes, take ownership for it, and try to fix it.

2) As I discussed other people's relationships, some say I may be desperate. Though I'm not, what I am doing is what I should have done all along. The one thing I learned really hard is to be honest with how you feel and what you want because you will never love properly when you hold back because of fears. That you need to bring your pride down to love. I think both of us could have been more direct without trying to give hints of what we want. To express our intentions directly, to be less prideful.

3) I am mature, but also immature in other parts of life. It is important to show you by my actions that I've grown and the willingness to take the leap of growth. My growth in learning to be honest in my feelings, which I think I have already grown a lot as I have become more open with my family and you. My growth in facing my fears and taking a risk and not bailing. We both speak two different love languages and we express love differently. I think you express love through action

and physical touch. Thus, I need to learn how to show you love your way.

- Am I correct? How have I shown you love?

4) I realized that you were also my motivation, I just never saw it until I lost it. The reason I can do the distance is the reason I work so hard in school. The feeling of making someone happy, and to show them your effort and love. It makes me happy at least to know that we were that. We gave that feeling to push ourselves forward.

5) The amount of patience you had with me and I didn't give you enough of it. I have many excuses for why I didn't, but I never recognized my impatience. This is my time now in this break to give you the patience you will need.

6) I have been living not enough for us (or trying hard enough). So maybe this is the leap I need to take now for us rather than later in the future.

- You told me last time that you can reflect all you want in a soccer match after it's over, but it's over. Though don't you play the game again with your team? You take your mistakes and you win the next game.

7) When you told me that your friends also agreed with you to ask for space and you said you didn't really care, I had to think about that as I do talk to my friends too and try to get a fresh perspective, but also I do know sometimes it can get into your head. That only you know the truth between me and you and this relationship. What you did and how we treated each

other, I had to reflect as the third person, but to be able to see both sides of the whole story.

- Ask yourself questions as if you were the reader of our story.

8) We talked a little about our limitations and everyone has limitations stacked against them. I agree you and I have limitations and your limitation is your career, but I knew that, that as a researcher you will always be in contracts until you become a professor. I knew that I took that risk and still want to.

- How have you been a limitation to me?

I realized that we both didn't give each other fair opportunities to show how much we really love each other. This space we have given each other is our second chance of a fair opportunity to show how much we do love each other. We are taking a risk together by working hard on ourselves for our relationship without certainty. Now that is real effort.

There are two more things I would like you to work on and that is being honest with your feelings and expressing your intentions, without expecting others to take your hint. I want you to be curious about the relationship and ask questions to yourself and me and discuss it together. I think all I need from you as we continue this journey on our break is your faith in me that we can overcome this. I have faith in you. This break is good. Sometimes you need space to appreciate each other. In our future we will need to continue to change ourselves as we grow or change in our life.

Learning from things like this will help our relationship grow. To tackle problems better and take what we learned to guide our relationship. What should have we done instead? I can't do this on my own and need to know that you are also growing yourself. To take this break, but to know that we believe in each other in our growth. I reflect later when you are ready and reflect in a natural time. When your fears are calm, but you aren't overly excited. When you are ready to share let me know. As we continue our long term assessment I hope we continue to grow. I just want to love you better.

I love you,
Your Guapa

Dear Guapo,

Throughout my lost relationships I had with friends, flings, and my first love, my heart never physically hurt the way it has been hurting. We haven't even broken up and are in a space, but knowing that I could lose you made my heart hurt. It is honestly the weirdest feeling like a numbness, a ting or a slight pull as your heart contracts. However, when I admit the feeling that I have of regret my heart comes to an ease knowing that this must be the truth. As I reflected as a third person I realized how much pain I have caused you and for that I am sorry. This feeling of regret, is it because I hate myself for the pain I created or what could have been?

I know that I can't take back what I did and it is in the past, but I can move forward and create a new future.

For the past four years I planned my future with you, during this time a part of me felt lost because you were my future home. I had to think back at nineteen years old and figure out what I would have done if I wasn't with you. All I know is that I always wanted to travel, explore and be a teacher. I have become a different person with different goals now. I had so much growth from you and I love the person I am today because you help me shape that. As I said before you gave me the experiences to grow, but it is how I took those experiences that made me become the person I am today. This itself is an experience for me to grow. Thank you.

It took me a while to reflect on regret and to me it is not a reminder of what I did wrong and to hate myself over it, but knowing I could do better. This space is hurting me a lot because I don't know if I will ever get to show you how good I can love you with learning through mistakes together. I want to love you better as we grow in our relationship and face any problem together and learn from our mistakes and how to face those problems. I decided I am going to move back to London in September as a biology teacher.

I know you have decided to work on your own career, and continue doing that for yourself. This is your self growth and the biggest limitation that I think you need to face yourself. Your vocation is the only thing I will never be able to help you directly with, but I can support you indirectly. Your instability was/is my biggest limitation. I also think you can work on making less excuses for yourself, take your experience that you have gone through and find the light in things rather than be negative. Don't be afraid to experience things a second time. You may not know what may come from it. Find your balance in being a dreamer again, but also be realistic.

My reason for London is simply taking a leap by trying to work on our relationship and myself. For myself I know I will not regret whatever the outcome will be because this is me trying my best. As long as I know I have tried my best and I did everything I could in the relationship to fix what I did wrong, I will have no regrets on how this relationship goes. I'll leave it up to faith and faith in you to take it from there. The first lesson I learned in our relationship. As I'm learning to be patient with you this time and with myself. You are going through a lot and I understand that, and in every relationship there are going to be times when one partner will need to work harder than the other. For now I'm willing to do that until either one of us breaks or closes the spaces. There are so many questions I want to ask you myself in person, but I know you are not in the right space or mindset for it.

Yours,
Guapa

Dear Mom,

I know that this choice I will be picking will hurt you and I am sorry. Even though I know I will hurt you, I know you will always support me and have my back. This is what unconditional love is. I am sorry that I will be taking advantage of that and be taking that for granted. However, I think our time apart has made us grow so much. I never felt more connected to you before. I never felt so honest with you ever before. I always feared to make you and Dad worried. I always hid a lot of my feelings and stuff because I didn't want to make you worry. Though this year I realized it's okay to make you and Dad worry and that you will understand and hold me. I also know not to take that for granted as I also want to be as independent as I can. Though it's okay to find balance between the two. I know you only care and want the best for me and that you will tell me certain things to do. I understand so much more of you, Mom, and the reasoning behind so much of your pain and your relationship with Dad after experiencing heartbreak myself.

Through my own experience I get to connect with you, Mom. I'm also realistic, which is something that you have instilled in me. I'm going back to London, but with the mistakes I learned, I'm not gonna just pick the first school. I know the questions I need to ask to make sure that school is fit for me. I can't keep getting babied by my fears; I need to face this head on. Sadly, Mom, I will need to suffer more in life even if you don't want me too. However, you did raise me to be a strong woman, a woman who never gives up and knows how to at least provide for herself. You gave me so much, but now I need to use what you gave me to face my fears and challenges. I do regret my decision, Mom, and I know I don't want to live with regret, but I do know this year if nothing works out with him then that is his loss not mine any more.

This year will be different because I don't know what will happen next year. I have no plans for next year. I told you that my whole life I have been planning and working hard towards my goals. From high school joining all these clubs to make sure I got into university and increased my chance of going into med school. I never told you and Dad, but in my first year of university I did already know I wanted to be a teacher and go abroad. I continued to work hard on my degree because I thought it was important for me to have more education and not limit myself. This year after ten years I will have no plan for next year and will take it as I go. I know that even if I have no plan for next year I do know that I will get experience for my career and still be able to have all the opportunities in the world.

One thing I know for sure is that I am happy to know I can go anywhere in the world and be able to do what I love, but I just don't know where that feeling of home is yet. Your home will always be my roots and where I came from, but I also need to find my own home. Toronto I know isn't my home and I need to travel more to find it. It may take me a while, but for now I know I will be coming back to your home in a year. I made sure to only pack one suitcase and a bag.

I love you,

Your daughter.

Lesson Eighteen: Get out of your head

Ironic again how here I am writing and talking to myself in my own little brain. There are so many times within the break that I have gone back to the destructive self by listening to my fears and getting inside my own head. Wondering why he didn't respond? Did I ruin the conversation? Is our connection gone? Does he still love me? Is he seeing other people? This is where I could grow to remind myself of lessons and repeat in my mind. That eventually by saying it and repeating it, it would become a part of me. This is the part of life that is hard it is to unlearn, learn, and relearn, our own ideas and theories. Though with those moments when we go back to our older selves we need to use those moments to practice our new thoughts and ideas. Another reason for me to write this book was for me to have my new concept of me written in words. That by writing it I must now live by it and try my best to not be hypocritical to the concept that I will now be living by. This will take time, patience, but everyone once in a while can be a hypocrite; it's something that we all do. Though it is important to catch yourself and recognize it so you don't go back. When you reflect, ask yourself neutral questions about yourself rather than others. Reflecting can go wrong when you think negatively about yourself or think negative thoughts. It is important to find a good moment for your reflection. When you start to lead yourself towards negative thoughts, that's when it doesn't become reflecting. That's when you need to get out of your own head when you are between hope and fear.

July: Pain, Sadness, Anger, Frustration, ~~Freedom?~~

During the months of May and June I felt sadness, the pain of maybe losing something, the pain of fighting for something alone, the pain of lost hope, the pain and disappointment of myself. I was sad and in pain because I didn't want to lose someone important. I'd already made the decision to go back to London, found a job and found a nice studio apartment for myself.

However, in July that started to change. I felt anger towards him. The reasoning for his break just seemed involved, it felt more like assumptions rather than real reasoning to end a four year relationship. Seeing the lack of progress on things that he needed to work on frustrated me. The fact that with any problems I had I always talked about it. Either it be a conversation or an argument, but never out of the blue ending of a relationship. It was ending a relationship without even trying to work out some solution that made me angry.

I had a lot of anger in July and I needed to ask myself again some questions about my feelings. Was this frustration directed at him? Was I mad at him for his actions or the way it was handled? I wanted to have a conversation and ask questions to find answers. I realized that I was angry and frustrated because I couldn't understand him. Not at him or myself, but the lack of connection from not understanding one another. I think that's where frustration and anger comes from in a relationship. It is not being understood or not being able to understand. Similar to those stupid word problems in math, always trying to solve for x, we just don't get it.

At one point I wondered did I still love him. Was I telling myself I didn't love him to make this easier for me to be calm about our new communication rule of texting once a week? Was this a white lie to keep my sanity? You know telling yourself something and eventually it will come true even if it was a lie. Could that be possible? From holding it in and being afraid to say I love you. That I was trying to replace it with indifference.

There were moments when I woke up and missed him and then there were moments when I woke up and was like I don't care any more. Did I care if he said no at the end of September, that we weren't getting back together? That I quit my job and moved back to a school system I couldn't handle in the past? The answer was no, but I think I was viewing this move now differently. At first it was a new chance at love with him, but no matter how it went it would be a new chance for something else.

I put a lot of effort in, in May and June, caring for him still and wanting to not have his love for me die out.

Was hope enough to keep someone loving? I still loved him, but my love was wavering.

In a way I was slowly embracing the freedom of attachment. The freedom of just only worrying about yourself is a lot easier, but when there is freedom of attachment will there be longing? Freedom is an interesting word as there is no such thing as complete freedom. Even if you think about freedom not on a personal level, but in society. There is no real freedom as we have laws to protect us, it restrains us, but we decided to give up some freedoms to gain others. If we had absolute freedom as humans could we truly be able to handle it? For me I realized that there are different types of freedom and it is choosing which freedom you want in your life. Maybe it is because of choice that we are stuck without absolute freedom? All I know, is that we have choices to make and I needed to question the choice of love. I was questioning the freedom of love and loneliness, that love frees us from loneliness, but the consequence of it is adding more restrictions in our life. Is it worth it? The question was did I want the freedom of responsibility of another person's life in exchange for the freedom of loneliness? Or is this concept not true at all, maybe love is actually an absolute form of freedom?

Lesson Nineteen: Question your feelings

Your feelings play a huge part in your everyday life because they play on our choices in life. There's the rational decision making process, which is easy to make in scenes of pros and cons and making probable guesses on the outcome of a choice. Feelings are hard because we always want to make a decision that will avoid negative feelings and increase positive feelings. Thus, it is really important to ask yourself questions about the feeling from not just why do I feel this way, but when did I feel this way? What or who made me feel this way? How did these feelings come to be? We may not like to admit it, but our feelings at the end of day will outweigh our logical decisions even if we like it or not. It's how we look at the pros and cons and the feelings we weigh on it as negative or positive.

For me I need to question before acting and hold off a lot of messaging and communication towards him. Was this a conversation I wanted to have, which was erected by my emotions? That was a choice I needed to make, which was to message him or not. How to respond to his message was also a choice I needed to make. This feeling of indifference was something I needed to question deeply and if it was truly indifference before I made a choice to end the relationship. Did my love fade enough for me to choose the freedom from attachment? He asked me once that I should ask myself , "What would I do without him?" I thought about it and answered that I could do many of the same things with a different person. The question he should have told me to ask myself is, "What would I miss about him?" I would miss him teaching me about the concept of life.

Him

I wanted to understand him from what was on his mind to who he was as a person. I have become less blinded by love, but can now see who he truly was. I always thought that he was a good person and that it gave me the courage to have trust and respect. With trust that he would be a committed, kind, caring, and understanding person. Though when I talked to my friends about the things he has said or wrote to me they thought he was jealous of me, that he held resentment in himself. I told them that he never seemed like a jealous person, but when I think about when someone enters a dark place anything can happen. As I said he was a good person, but that doesn't mean he will never have those dark moments. That was where love blinded me and a reminder that he could have those moments even when you wish it to not be true.

We did text each other and still communicated with each other during the break as that was one of our conditions of free communication. Though in the middle of June we stopped texting regularly and it started with him writing to me "Have a good week." For me I understood this as I don't mind talking to you, but I want it less, which I respect. I stopped texting him and eventually stopped updating him about my life. He would text me every week asking me how my week went. I would respond with a lot of information and ask more questions. Though he would respond and still entertain me, which confused me even more. Why would he text me if he didn't want to converse with me? What was his intention? I tried to ask, but that just made him more annoyed by my questions. It is hard to understand someone when they aren't willing to express themselves honestly. The best thing you can do is explain your intentions, step back and give space.

Honestly, was he just as much as I was? Our relationship was complicated, and there were insecurities because our relationship was not stable at that moment. Who knew what we would decide in September as new feelings, our understanding of love, the relationship, and ourselves. Was he checking in to see how I was doing out of kindness? Was he checking to be reassured by his feelings of the current break? The nervousness of the change as we were starting to get used to this new normal without each other?

We talked again mid-July. He told me what I never thought was possible. I always tried to make him know that I believed and always wanted to support his dreams. Though he told me my support was doing the opposite, making him lose his self-esteem. He told me he had expressed this to me, but I think I just didn't interpret it correctly. I wanted to be together, and if I needed to support him until he could support himself, I was willing to do that. These things take time, and I knew that. What he saw in himself was sad, but what I saw was a man trying his best.

You would think the longer you have been with someone, the better you get to know them, but even though I had known him for four years, I couldn't give a good answer to these questions using what I knew of him. I think it was hard because I didn't know his current state. Was this the new him or a moment passing? Thus, no matter how long you think you know someone for you are always learning so much more about them.

Lesson Twenty: Listen

This whole time I've been talking about questioning others to understand. This is correct, when I ask further questions I do get further into understanding more, but why? Why did I keep asking questions to understand? Simple because when I listened the first time, I couldn't make a logical interpretation of what was being said. Thus, listening is as essential as asking questions. That may be that time when I kept asking him questions, and he felt annoyed because I wasn't listening. That perhaps deep down, I would get my answer from my questions from just listening. Thus, to listen is to understand, but to question is to know if you followed the first time. So taking this new concept of listening, remember to listen to every answer to your question. Even listening to those questions with no explanation, listen to the silence because even that can speak words.

August

Remember when I said that I had a lot of questions, but I was still waiting for the right time. I felt that the conversation in mid-July made me reflect more and have even more questions. As I was preparing for what I wanted to say in September, I came to a stop myself and asked why am I waiting. Is it not the right time? What makes something the right time? Is there really such thing as a right time or is that us making excuses? Is it to hide behind what is true until we are really ready to accept it? Yes, I am working on patience with myself and I should be patient to ask my questions. I thought all those deep questions and reflections would be discussed in September. Honestly, that could be overwhelming. What was holding me back? Simple, it was the fear of the reaction. I think I always have these questions, but I fear the reaction. Why did I worry when I didn't have anything to lose any more? I had already accepted the possibility that our relationship could end. So I decided to ask to Skype more regularly to answer my questions.

I wanted to make this move to London different than the last time. My mom told me that she felt that I was going and doing the same thing. However, I felt like

I wasn't this time; I was going with more experiences. I was going to be a high school teacher, which I never did before, but was an opportunity for me to explore and mould myself into something different. I found a lovely studio just under an hour's walk from my school. It had these tall, beautiful Victorian windows that brought light to the room. It wasn't one of those cramped places where when you walked two steps and there was the toilet. Though I only had a small closet and a drawer I knew before going to London, I would need to minimize my lifestyle. So I Maria Kondo'd the shit out of my things and minimized my life to thirty-three items before I left. Now, this was difficult. It took me like fifty times to pack and unpack my suitcase as I loved everything. I was learning to let go of my things, to be grateful for what they provided me. Maybe prepearing me to let go of him.

As I paid for my first month's rent and was left alone, I looked around my studio, and I knew I needed to embrace this moment. I took a deep breath at six a.m., looking at the sunrise from my studio apartment, and I finally accomplished one of my goals, which was to live alone. I got to decorate the place and make it my own. I was taking a step into one of my purposes, which was trying to find a home, and here I was making my own physical home and anything I wanted it to be. Though I still needed to find the answer to what makes the feeling of a home to me.

I also decided after settling down to go off to Greece by myself. I have flown on airplanes by myself, but never really explored by myself for more than a day in another country alone. I didn't need to see him in Spain, and I was able to spend my money in a place I always wanted to go and see. I booked a bike, hiking and cooking tours as those are my favourite things to do when travelling. It was nice doing the things I liked without worrying and caring about what others minded.

As I walked along the ocean, looking out into the sea, as the wind brushed around my skin and kissed my hair, I wondered what I would say to him when we met. I looked out to the ocean for answers. I sat down on my beach mat and took out my computer and started writing. I knew there was so much to say, and I didn't know where to start.

Lesson 21: Choice

This is where we have the free will to change our destiny. Life will give you a situation, and you are standing there, deciding what choices you have to deal with the situation. Yes, there are conditions in every choice, but at the end of the day, you choose that choice. As a hyper-analytical person, I don't just look at the facts, pros, and cons, but my feelings, why I feel more guided towards those choices than the other ones. This is what I wanted to explain to him, that my choices are based on my fears, some of my own upbringing, my morals, and at times others. I think something I learned is that before deciding to get hurt by someone's choice, maybe ask, "Why did you pick that choice?" Before we think about someone's decision as selfless, ask yourself, "Would I have done the same thing?". To also ask yourself, "Did I do the same thing for the person?" when you would have liked that person to have acted differently. That there is so much sub-information behind a choice. We all know a choice will change your life because it has consequences. We are choosing what consequences we want and the possible outcome of pain. However, there are limits to this idea for us who don't have a choice to choose.

That picking a choice isn't just in the moment, but also one's consideration into the future and reflecting on their past lessons. A decision of choice defines who that person is at the moment. The consequences of a choice tell us who that person is becoming. How we want to come to understand this choice is our perception of it. Be honest with what it means and own up to our choices and the reasons behind it because it will become us in the past and future.

My past affected my decision on why I wanted this relationship to work. My past relationship with my ex was this amazing man. He taught me a lot, and I always wonder what we could have been. Though he ended up finding his one, so obviously he wasn't mine. My ex taught me about knowing yourself and your limitations. I'm actually still very good friends with my last ex.

I wanted to try my best and to drop all of my fears of uncertainty and judgement that had been holding me back. If I continued this relationship with him, there was going to be a lot of healing to do and re-connecting our love. This was going to take a lot of work, also reflecting on what needed to change, what we needed to work on ourselves and how we would support each other. I had already moved my ass to another country, was this really going to stop me now? My past shows me as someone who is learning from their mistakes and taking a step in trying to be their best self. My future is showing me as someone who knows her current self and the challenges ahead. So who am I at this moment? Hopefully, I've always been optimistic.

The Future

Dear Future Me,

You have grown so much in the past four years. Yes, some of it has to do with him, but it is also essential to know how you also led to your growth. He gave you the experiences to grow, but it is how you took those experiences that made you become the person you are today. You didn't let anything negative take you down, you pushed forward with a positive mindset and always tried to find new solutions. Sadly, this is because your whole life was to prove people wrong, but you now have a beautiful, positive, resilient mind. You have grown up never to be a quitter. You know the struggles of life and the injustices in this world, but you always find a way to bring light to things. To change perspective in such a positive way, to make people want to do good for others and themselves. Your humour to laugh at yourself, to know that you messed up, to criticize yourself, but even to know your true worth. This is something that you should never change as I think it was one of your best qualities, accepting you are only human.

We have faced many of our fears, but our worries never indeed go away even when we have conquered them in one moment in our life. Fears have a way to always come back around, and we must be careful when they do. Fear is there to protect us, but it can also be there to hinder us. We must prepare ourselves for our fears, so when we are ready, we can leap.

I have noticed that every concern I have felt was resolved by being honest with ourselves and people. The fear of disappointing my loved ones. I opened to my mom about that fear and being told that I would never disappoint her brought relief to me. From that, I learned that if it is unconditional love that people will accept our mistakes and watch us grow. The fear of being myself. Being able to open about my learning disability to him was my first step in being myself. That people who love me or care will accept me no matter what issues I have. New fears also can appear in life, but we need to recognize them and face them honestly. The fear of telling him you love him, but he doesn't. The fear of losing him as anyone does with their partner, for four years is hard. This is time for me to practice my patience with myself, when I am ready and prepared to be honest with him about that fear, but whatever happens, I will be okay. I have done such courageous things already, and I will survive. Take it slow; it's okay to slow down. It will not be as bad as it seems. I will end this letter with three other lessons so far:

Lesson 22: Change

Throughout these four years together, as I reflected on myself, I notice that I have changed and that he has changed. The most exciting thing about human relationships is the way they change over time. The person I love today, will not be the same person I love ten years down the road. The hard part of love can grow together, yet to also expand to find our true self at the same time. As we live, change is inevitable as our environment and surroundings change around us, and it is only natural we change as well. Though how we change, and grow is dependent on us and what we take from your experiences. Sometimes life gets us busy, and we forget to stop and reflect. Don't forget to sit back and reflect on your day. As I wrote this book, I learned every day, you have a moment, and it is taking the time to reflect on them. Don't wait to reflect on your actions because those little actions can grow into something big. It's better to recognize earlier rather than later because you will have to face it anyway eventually. It is easier to deal with smaller problems than a big one. Once a week, sit back and reflect on how you feel, what you noticed about the world and the things you are worried about.

Lesson 23: Life

The stories of others helped me gain courage and made me realize that everyone's life story is different. It made me feel less scared of my own life and the path that it will or may take. Listening to them without judgement and asking questions about their experiences and how it made them feel, what made them feel a certain way, and how their feelings have changed, helped me understand my own life. Though a lot of stories we talked about didn't all end in happy endings, it somehow made me feel less worried about the uncertainty of life. Knowing that these individuals all had uncertainty in their life and still do, but they keep on going. Life is a paradox, and no matter how many philosophers try to understand life, we will never truly find a definite answer to life, aporia.

If there is one thing I know, life is hard for everyone, but it is a lot easier when you just try to be a "good person". Now when I mean good I don't mean perfect. What I mean is that you tried your best to be whatever a good person is to you. For me it just means I was decent, fair and kind. I think also realizing we are all hyprocrites. For me to judge someone's actions to even be mad at someones actions is to really consider "Have I done that myself?" I have been asking myself every day these past few months, "Was I a good person today?" "Is this what a good person is?" "Would a good person understand?" "How would a good person react?"

This concept of the good person is how I perceive the person I want to be in the future, and isn't life about becoming your best self? I want my best self to be someone who can project when they feel uncomfortable in a respectful and assertive way because kindness is key to both myself and others.

Lesson 24: Know to let go

It is essential to fight for what you want, but it is also important to know when you lost the fight. Eventually, it is finding out if he is still willing to fight with you and keep knocking down the hurdles in this relationship. Though you did your very best in this relationship deep down, this was your best. You will find someone who has the strong will that you have or even greater, the willingness to change for themselves, and the effort to fight with you even when life throws you shit. You must find a fighter as strong and powerful as yourself.

Love,
Past Self

Leap

Dear Readers,

Thank you for reading this book. As I wrote this book, I had to place myself in your shoes. How will this book change me? What answers and questions am I hoping to find? As I said in the beginning, you may not get any answers for what you may be looking for, but I hope you found it. For me the purpose of the book was to give readers the feeling of calm even when not knowing an outcome of something. To change the anxiousness of fear and the uncomfortablness of change. Fear is powerful but so are curiosity, love, and hope. You have so many things up against fear, so remember its three against one.

I still do not know where my story is heading: does he end it with me or will my move show him my ultimate sacrifices? Though with all the crap everyone goes through I know one thing: I will be fine. I feel that I'm still afraid of many things, but I think I'm willing to face them more quickly because life isn't waiting for you. Don't hold yourself back from exploring every possible thing even if it may feel like it will kill us because where would be heading? As humans, we naturally search for answers; we go through elenchus with our inner selves or with others, we always reach a state of aporia. Our brain is powerful and beautiful, but it also has limitations in which we do not have access to the whole spectrum of realities and truths at a point in time, so we can only adapt by uneven steps. That we are all taking these uneven steps towards something unknown, it may not even be the answers that we are going towards. We don't know until we get there, and instead of keeping your expectations high for the end of the journey of something unknown, leap.

The reason I named this *book Leap* was not that I was taking a chance on something, but the power of where you can leap. You can leap forward, backwards, left, or right, in any direction. It is not linear; you can explore the complex dimension of this vast space called life. Leap forward and grow, leap left or right to change your path, if it goes wrong, you can always leap backwards. I decided not to describe the character or give them a name, as this is a true story. I wanted you guys as readers to embody the character as much as possible to feel like you were having that inner dialogue with yourself as you read the book. I only have one question left for you: Are you going to leap?

With much love,

Ting Ting